The Dandelion Seed

By Joseph Anthony
Illustrated by
Cris Arbo

DAWN Publications

For all dandelion seeds,
especially you.
—JA & CA

Publisher's Cataloging-in-Publication (Provided by Quality Books, Inc.)

Anthony, Joseph Patrick
        The dandelion seed/by Joseph Anthony;
illustrated by Cris Arbo. — 1ˢᵗ ed.
        p. cm.
        ISBN: 1-883220-66-1 (hardcover)
        ISBN: 1-883220-67-X (softcover)

1. Dandelions — Juvenile fiction. 2. Seeds — Juvenile fiction.
I. Arbo, Cris. II. Title.

PZ7.A58Da 1998   [E]
                        QBI97-40481

Dawn Publications
12402 Bitney Springs Rd
Nevada City, CA 95959
800-545-7475
nature@DawnPub.com

Manufactured by Regent Publishing Services, HongKong Printed July, 2019 in ShenZhen, Guangdong, China
25 24 23

First Edition

Designed by LeeAnn Brook Design

I t was autumn in the garden.
All the flowers had died
and dropped their seeds.

Only one seed was left, a little dandelion seed who was afraid to let go.

But the winter wind began to blow. The stronger the wind blew, the tighter the seed hung on until it felt the wind blowing right through it.

Then the seed left the garden behind.
It became part of the wind, and
was carried away.

The world was bigger than
the seed ever imagined.

It was also more frightening,

more lonely,

and more beautiful.

The more the seed saw,
the smaller it felt.

It wondered where it belonged.

The seed landed when snow began to fall. It listened in silence as peace covered it like a blanket.

Finally spring came. Sunshine warmed the air and the soil, and the little seed began to grow tiny leaves and roots.

Its leaves spread wide
to gather sunlight.

Its roots reached deep
to drink fresh rain.

Soon the seed flowered into the bright, delicate dandelion it was meant to be.

It shared its green leaves
with deer and rabbits.

I

t gave sweet nectar to
bees and butterflies.

Then, almost overnight, the life that began as one little dandelion seed ripened into many. They each became part of the wind, and were carried away.

All except one.

"Don't be afraid," whispered the dandelion.
"The wind and the sun and the
rain will take care of you.
Let go and you will see."

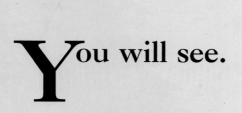

You will see.

As well as tapping inspiration from within, Joseph Anthony draws from a smorgasbord of life experiences. His work as a corrections officer, a traveling musician in the U.S. Navy, a massage therapist, a carpenter, and a natural food store clerk have all served to deepen Joseph's understanding of himself and his connection with dandelions. He lives with his children and his wife, Cris Arbo, in Buckingham, Virginia.

Versatile across the artistic spectrum, Cris Arbo has worked as art director for London's Dance Centre, and as a vocalist with the London Symphony and the London Philharmonic. Her art, inspired by a love and respect for nature, is known for intense details and is created by hand with paints and pencils, without the use of a computer. She has also worked as a background artist, tracer and painter for animated feature films and television. Her most prized works are her children: Lisi, Julie, Arianna and Alina.

Other Books Illustrated by Cris Arbo

The Dandelion Seed's Big Dream by Joseph Anthony. After 17 years the dandelion seed has returned in this charming tale of a seed that encounters all sorts of obstacles and opportunities—this time of the urban kind.

What's in the Garden? by Marianne Berkes. Good food doesn't begin on a store shelf in a box. It comes from a garden bursting with life. Healthy fruits and vegetables become much more interesting when children know where they come from. And a few tasty recipes can start a lifetime of good eating.

In the Trees, Honey Bees by Lori Mortensen offers an inside-the-hive view of a wild colony, along with solid information about these remarkable and valuable creatures.

In a Nutshell by Joseph Anthony. Who we are. Why we are here. Where we come from and where we go. Every child ponders life's greatest questions. Here, in a nutshell, is a tale about life.

Other distinctive nature awareness books from Dawn Publications

Octopus Escapes Again!—Swim along with Octopus as she leaves the safety of her den to search for food. She outwits dangerous enemies by using a dazzling display of defenses.

Daytime Nighttime, All Through the Year—Rhyming verses introduce young children to three science concepts—the seasons of the year, animal behavior, and nocturnal animals. Two animals are depicted for each month, one that is active during the day and one that is active during the night.

A Moon of My Own — An adventurous young girl journeys around the world accompanied by her faithful companion, the Moon. Wonder and beauty await you.

Pitter and Patter — Take a ride a water cycle with Pitter and Patter, two drops of water! You'll go through a watershed, down, around, and up again. Oh, the places you'll go . . .

The Mouse in the Meadow — A curious young mouse boldly ventures into the meadow. There he gets a crash course about life from creatures both friendly and not so friendly.

Seashells by the Seashore—What works of art are shells! A lovely lilting rhyme takes children on a walk on the beach discovering beautiful shells along the way.

Granny's Clan—Life as a wild orca (killer) whale is a family affair. Here is the true story of Granny, a 100 year-old whale matriarch, who teaches young whales and helps her magnificent clan to survive.

Dawn Publications is dedicated to inspiring in children a deeper understanding and appreciation for all life on Earth. You can browse through our titles, download resources for teachers, and order at www.dawnpub.com, or call 800-545-7475.